Sophia's
Poems

Biblioteca Euskal Erria
Serie diáspora, No. 4

Sophia's Poems

Sophia Dominga Etxeberria

Euskal Erria

Montevideo
2015

Biblioteca Euskal Erria
Serie diáspora, No. 4

Biblioteca Euskal Erria
    Solano García 2643/101,
    CP 11300,
    Montevideo, Uruguay
    Tel.: 00598 2908 7977

Copyright © 2015 Biblioteca Euskal Erria

Eskubide guztiak erreserbatuak. Egilearen edo editoreen baimenik gabe liburuaren erreprodukzio osoa edo partziala zein kopia, erabilera, distribuzioa, komertzializazioa eta komunikazio publikoa (besteak beste) debekatuta dago.

All rights reserved. No part of this publication may be reproduced, stored in a retrieval system, or transmitted, in any form or by any means, electronic, mechanical, photocopying, recording or otherwise, without the prior permission of the series editor and the author.

First edition. First print
Printed in America

Cover design © 2015 JSM

ISBN-10 first edition: 0692527494
ISBN-13 first edition: 978-0692527498

by Sophia Dominga Etxeberria

To my father, Domingo Etxeberria

>   Ghosts
>   hide in the sea,
>   in stars,
>   in every leaf
>   falling…

Contents

Sophia	15
I Am an American Basque	17
Confusion	18
Temeroso	19
Stardust	20
Black sky	21
White	22
Dream the night stream	23
Dragonfly Express	24
The train to Buenos Aires	26
Zunico	28
Tentative connection	29
Club Hípico	30
Counting the hours	31
Beneath Pluto and the street lamp	32
Florencio	33
Revolution Girls	34
Carta de Santiago	35
For Randall Crawford	36
The orphan	37

One night in Arkansas	38
Reverence for the good	39
American Skyline	40
Forget winter	42
Breakfast in Jackson	43
Jokaldi	44
Gold	45
Esposo	46
Heat	48
Break Point	49
Tradition of evening	50
Pain	52
September	53
Petradom weather	54
Smoke of dusk	56
Ghost Dance	57
The long good-bye	58
Mr. Sever's trees	59
The Circus (after reading The Garden by Ezra Pound)	60
Adios	61
X	62
Samba	63
On the eve of destruction	64
The storm	65

A serious chat	66
Date at the carnival by the sea	67
Sustenance	68
Captain Logan's Paradox	70
Justo y la luna en el río de La Plata	71
Jackpot Nevada	72
The name game	73
The mathematician's cave	74
Hologram	75
What a woman wants	76
To my brother at sea	77
Argentina	78
Happy birthday baby	80
Flamenco	82
Bengal tea	83
Saratoga	84
Gernika	85
Tumpa	86
Remembering Jesus and…	88
Tierra de mi padre	90
Sunchabamba	91
Excommunication	92
Zeru aingeru (heavenly angel)	93
Nothing more than this	94
The measure of all things	95

Alone	96
A rough idea	97
Wind rod	98
Mantorni	99
In another language	100
The shore	101
Paco de Lucia	102
Melody of Cordoba	103
Touch the body	104
Ramon	105
Señor Barrutia's reply	106
Guardian of night	107
Piña de agave	108
Toro bravo	109
Snap and break	110
Dreaming the Yellowstone	112
Except for this	113
Here comes misery	114
Shipwrecked	115
Shanaz	116
The smoking lounge	117
Quiet the mind	118
Death by chocolate	119
Piura	120
Graywacke	122

Dobbertin	124
The light from your window	125
Swimming in the hearts of saints	126
A letter from the black virgin	127
Nietzsche is my boyfriend	128
No! Nietzsche is my boyfriend!	130
Lullaby for a Buddhist monk	131
Father Ortiz	132
Father Ortiz goes grocery shopping	133
Father Ortiz at the car wash	134
Father Ortiz in the office of the bishop	135
Quepos	136
Return to blue	137
Sai rom	138
Colorado (for Vincent)	139
Iñaki	140
A letter home	141
Sphere	142
Smile of your memory	144
Sometimes you have to go far away to write a love poem	146
For Xabier-2013	147
In search of God and Haiku	148
The bullfight	149

Sophia

Sophia Dominga Etxeberria is a dancer, a singer and a poet. She was born and raised in a large Basque sheep ranching family in the Western United States.

Her father, Dr. Dom Etxeberria, was born in Auritz-Burguete, in Navarre, the Basque Country, in 1925. His parents immigrated to the United States and became sheep ranchers in Arizona where they raised their eleven children. Dom joined the navy in 1942 where he trained to be a dentist and a pilot. WWII came to an end before he served. He married Sophia's mother, Sophie Fletcher Burden in 1948.

He graduated from Colorado State University with a degree in Veterinary Medicine, DVM, in 1953. In 1956 he was hired to work for the Eisenhower Administration in a program designed to help South American countries improve agricultural conditions.

He moved his wife and four children to the Andes Mountains in Peru and then traveled to many of the surrounding countries. In 1958 he returned to the U.S. to build a small empire of sheep, cattle, horses, and ranches in Colorado and Wyoming and to raise his family of seven children. He was killed in an auto accident outside of Goodland, Kansas, in 1970.

Poems

"His death created a doorway," said Sophia, "a path to follow-- and I did. For years I wandered in a strange world, sinking to the bottom of dark holes, crawling on my hands and knees, trying to find my way through the dark. And then I found poetry. One by one my poems illuminated a path back to the everyday world. It is true: The antithesis of depression is creativity."

She wrote these poems over a fifteen year period. She wrote in Argentina, Spain, the Basque Country, Wyoming, Arizona, California, the Grand Canyon and Colorado.

"I looked for him in the cante and baile of flamenco and in the Spanish and Basque languages. I caught glimpses of face, traces of his ghost. I studied the love letters he wrote to my mother from Peru. In the end I came up against the hugeness of the word "dead". I hope these poems will guide my father home and help him to find peace."

Sophia D. Etxeberria

I Am an American Basque

I was born in a country of dreamers
where they say anything is possible.
The Basques charted maps and built ships and sailed to the Americas

so I believed. I danced beneath a star
that hung near a crescent moon as
the world spread out before me, an unnamed prophet of the destroyed.

> Herri batean jaio nintzen
> Non edozein gauza posiblea dela esaten ohi dute.
> Euskal jatorrizkoa naiz ni,
> Euskal jendearen ondorengoa.
> Kartak zituzten nire arbasoek gordeta,
> Eta itsasoak zituzten nabigatu.
> Haiek bezala dantzan nago ni,
> Ilgoraren gainetik zintzilik doan izarpetan.
> Haiek bezala, mundu guztiari
> Zabalduta nator ni.

Confusion

In the dark, after turning out the lights,
you hate us, think our pain is ugly
that we are ugly. But we are not. We are disillusioned by the magnificence all around us. Monuments, skyscrapers, the wealth and dreams of America.

On our sheets, red and soft, we kick and bite with our arms around each other, mystified by the blue night and the reflection of our skin pale and glowing. The city lights, the dull glean
of green dollar bills mesmerizes us into awe so much so that when we examine our bodies we find our nakedness dull and uneventful.

But our skin, luminescent in the half moon light, shines beneath our little window to America. On this unmade bed we fold together with wounds and scars, tracing parts still tender, full of breath and touch, misunderstanding the intricacies, not fully appreciating the longitude and latitude of two confused American beauties.

Sophia D. Etxeberria

Temeroso

In the alley of fear I used
to worry about God,
devil language,
insanity, math
seductions
illusions
reality.

I worried my new lover, on a
moonlit night would find
my brain already
trained to wait
in the back
street
alley.

Laughter broke the spells
cast by the sociopath
and the narcissists.
Hard clear cold
sharp clean
flooding
dark all
to hell.

Stardust

The stark light of March
brushed against a shadow
high up in the eaves
where a dove built her nest
to sing about her loneliness.

He galloped on his horse,
somewhere far away. Was
it Uruguay where evening
held a promise of stars?
Every star is yesterday.

I wandered through a
memory of my father
where we were together
sitting on the couch as
he explained a death.

But not his own death.
His arms wrapped around
me as if stardust could
muffle the sound of crying
for a pet deer that was
dead and gone.

Sophia D. Etxeberria

Black Sky

The devil's hand reached out and choked
the sky, turned it inside out like a
stomach
of a poisoned cat,
squirming
inside the confines of its own skin,
gasping
to the end of it's last horrible day
before
the devil's work moved in the shadows below.

Black fog crept beneath his path, changed
from one form to another until tentacles
dangled from a funnel, pulsing and shivering
poised for murder, swirling slowly around
until they were swallowed by a dense
cloud
hovering in green. I have not seen you since.

White

"For nothing can be sole or whole that has not been rent."
William Butler Yeats

On every ray of sun light spread out
and sent the darkness whirling.

Shadows curled behind lampposts as
the church steeple received the sky.

Yes. The white horse died,
but white is not the "Whip of God!"

White fingers run through white hair.
White wool. White lover's magic.

White mushrooms. White fences. White linen.
White strands of pearls.

Forgiveness is white. White cloud
in bright blue of mid-day.

His truck was white, driving away.
Hope is white, too.

Sophia D. Etxeberria

Dream the night stream

Dream a turtle black and green
dream it small as crescent moon
Dream a turtle florescent breath
dream it floating light as seed

        Dream a sadness hibernating moon
        dream a moon light as breath
        dream a dandelion seed
            dreamed in the night stream

Dream a sadness old as rain
dream it loyal as a ring
Dream a sadness creek blue clear
dream hibernating deep and near

        Dream a turtle deep and green
        dream sadness round as a ring
        dream dandelions florescent green

Dream floating in deep lagoon

Dragonfly Express

Sewing beetles leave nothing to chance.
They chase their dreams
to out-lying walls of the future,
coolly ignoring the haunted
razor grass. Feudal lords,
noisy, dizzying, they twist
and dip in a psychedelic dance.
Traders. Envoys. They link
mystery and the center
of gravity.

At times they stumble through sky
or land on a window.
In a glimpse we capture
the cavernous urge to taste
something new. A volatile myopia.
We slip on our street shoes,
curve and swerve over
subterranean magma.

Sophia D. Etxeberria

Amid loneliness and boredom
we become ghostly forms
of mighty warriors tramping
through woods in search
of the dirty, the dangerous
the demanding. Hurtling
towards some remote destination
where we will be made mortal,
regain our stubborn,
cantankerous life full of color
and snap of the dragonfly
who sews our lips into a smile
behind blue veiled eyes
drifting in the gold atomic
dust of our origins.

The train to Buenos Aires

Ladislao Errazuriz's hollow eyes
leave the savage lair of humanity
fly the narrow road,
the narrow strait.
Clickety clack.
Clickety clack.

Questions are swept away
engulfed by chanting
girls and boys
from the oasis
of Santiago.
He is leaving.

Running. Torrents of light.
candles in a fever, descending
yet another lane amidst
myriad passages
of the deadly, dark game
of premature death.

So much to do. Learn the shape
of hands. Establish contact
with the Agency of Enshrined Bones.
Disperse the turmoil of the doorway.
Echoing: Claus Heileman
flicking his nails. Ships

Sophia D. Etxeberria

In the port of Valparaiso.
Maggots in the sheep of Laguna
Blanca. Empty rooms.
Echoing empty rooms.
Clickety
Clack

In the midst, typhoon
of sunburst. A bruised Christ closing
in on empires from East to West.
Casks of alter wine flowing.
In the brief case,
letter of resignation.
Clickety clack.
Clickety clack.

Zunico

I came to see you because of a dream.
The bells from the five o' clock mass
had not yet rung
and February seemed so far away.
Undoubtedly you think me
a lowly friend for having gone
so long without writing,
but the Zopilotes swooped down
from the bleached coast of Peru
and pecked at my words until
they were as dry as cherry
pits calling to the wind, "ooopa,
ooopa, ooopa." I'm sorry my friend,
so terribly sorry.

Softly, so as not to awaken anyone,
a lovely creature, a German girl
spoke to me in a peaceful language,
the language of night, the language
we understand and obey. She came to me like a seed blown
into a quiet pool.
But not until I stepped into her circle
of light, did I understand the word:
foreboding.

Sophia D. Etxeberria

Tentative connection

Rain clouds
evaporate
before touching Earth.
Taunt tingling saguaro
spines thirsting
from afar.
Owls loft messages
from distant canyons
in the company
of electric crickets
and elegant water.
Communicate subtle magic.
Wonder.
Was it their own voice heard,
or that of another?
Lizards
hide in sensitive cracks,
with glowing eyes
awakened
by the stirring
night wind
chasing javelina
through cholla.
Beneath moon,
beneath stars,
under the density of space
we await confirmation
of our tentative connection.

Club Hípico

I took the buttons off your jacket
and sewed them on my coat. I did
not offer them to anyone. I did not
explain or look back. I went to Club
Hipico where the caballeros were
drinking. I went like a sick horse
whose brain has begun to swell. I went
without assurance, without sanction,
without a picture of how beautiful you were to explain to all
the others about
why I was surrendering my advantage.

The girl behind the counter wanted
to hear my songs, to dance to them
during carnival. She was like pollen
rotting on the clefts of branches who
were losing their leaves. She too had
traveled with a man named Gutierrez.
I stayed until 11:30. We were yawning in each others' faces as
I wondered out loud how I would ever adapt to this small
world of chemical and electrical attractions I now called home.

Sophia D. Etxeberria

Counting the hours

There is a melancholy mood tonight
a breeze from Portugal
has taken my hand
and led me to a world forgotten ~
I had been happily dreaming
(until I received your sad letter.)

Oh! I live to ride my horse
to the water's mystery
to daydream and drift in rhythm
wandering through thoughts and
whispers no one needs to know
dreaming along the edge.

How happy you would be in Lima.
Does your skin still smell of thyme?
(such a sad letter)
caressing my hand while I walk,
wearing against my nerves, boldly
cascading over my soul with forgiveness.

Beneath Pluto and the street lamp

Tonight I will not jump
I will not despair
of being root bound.
Like the wind,
and everyone else
living on my block, I'll
slowly calm down,
drift into another night
of blessed sleep.

Sophia D. Etxeberria

Florencio

The Virgin of Pilar at Zaragoza
presides over her alter with the wings
of a wet dove. Never alone for a moment.
Suffocated by supplications and lamentations.
Like a black piglet stuffed into a sack
and slung over the shoulder.
of a man headed home for dinner,
She cries. About her son.

Still I take my prayers to her.
Prayers about rain. Prayers about
the pink rose deepening into purple
and your cricket, singing,
advising me not to repent.
I pray a little prayer to the Virgin
to watch over my letter, to take it
safely to your hand, to unfold my words.
I pray she looks away from sadness,
just for a moment, to see you dancing
like a schooner on the blue, blue sea.

Revolution Girls

My days, now, are mostly emptiness.
Cold. Vast. Remote.
Monday cannibalizes Tuesday.
Night consumes everything.
There are girls here in Peru.
They glow, form designs on beaches.
Revolutionize starlight.
But the afterglow is always you.

My trip to Huacrarucuo, delayed by
protestors in Shunchabamba, was
my last chance to capture
the low level pulse of the sky
who gleaned her clarity
from a crescent moon that
returned month after month
and then raced away to the

Andes who rose in temples
of carved dark solid matter
that silhouetted the ancient
distorted shock waves of
religions on beaches dancing
in firelight with thin, topless,
European mortal women
who drink coffee
at the café
in the morning.

Sophia D. Etxeberria

Carta de Santiago

Waves of green crumble
in lonely soil
still so madly in love

Pacific combers pound
loop through the unknown
gnaw at the reef and all of Chile

I saw your charmed eyes
slumped against extravagance
plotting your daring break

squatting on hot sand
my world was a grave
dying of nostalgia

wittingly or not, wind
probes desolation just as your
sleep flows in golden currents

For Randall Crawford

A light dusting of smoke on the coast and the holy
bells ringing
the shagged history of Argentina were doomed to
mingle along the
coastline. Bored with such talk I rode the gray mare
to the beach
on Sunday morning, where the rising sun tossed high
waves of cold
to the sand, wet and brown like the legs of a woman.
There is no reason for
certain things to survive.

And so you drifted down the Santiago River on a raft
from Ecuador
to Uruguay, a juicy plum roasting on a brazier of
glistening
heat, a fragment of a scent, an indiscernible noise.
How painful to
think of what passed between us. All cats are brown
after dark. And
now the roaring river carries its rocks to the shore
where nothing
is understood and the snow falls softly against my
ruin.

Sophia D. Etxeberria

The orphan

Summer dried up with the garden
and the clouds don't come to rain anymore.
Loneliness tumbles from the garbage truck;
after Halloween, every little pumpkin flame
has guttered out.
It is just me and coffee, me and cat,
me and this and that. I think if I
stare long enough at that tree over there
it will change into my father
and we will run away,
fast, fast, fast. But still no word.
Only the saints and the damned
write home on Sundays.

No. He is listening to the lake,
the lapping sound of waves breaking
over each pebble, each stone
of his horrible absence, that,
and the familiar music floating
from my mother's lips above a sink
full of soapy dishes.

One night in Arkansas

Here, this is where love hides,
in the filament of the south,
in the hum of the cricket,
where the storm seems to drop
lower and lower, scattering
the malcontents into the arms
of another.

And this is where it lives,
all across your face imprinted
with pain, washing me with bright wind,
so bright I look down. I look away.
I cry. I wait for the night to take
me into your bed,
to show me how to love you.

Love sleeps in the bloom of the poppy,
in the dark with my hands unseen.
The moon slips over the edge
and the night hawk breaths.
Silence falls before me like
buzzing petals,
like weeping dew
until I hear your footsteps.

Sophia D. Etxeberria

Reverence for the good

My husband is a sheep man.
And every day he walks Earth
his face in the sky, stars,
and the sun.
His hands touch
the wool
the sheep, the wool.
And at night
he comes home to me.
I breathe him,
the secret of my father,
my childhood,
our children,
his sex.

American Skyline

Skyscrapers exhibit a most complex social behavior
(in an artful way) - - chain copulation - -
they have sex with the sky all day long
in hermaphrodite mating orgies,
until clouds of purple explode,
and trillions of lights ejaculate
into blobs of mottled wild night.
Towers loll about, smoking in the afterglow.

Fastidious in detail, with rosy granite skin,
balanced
on the cutting edge of modern architecture.
Loved for their sexual maturity, they exist
by their definition of service:
corporate chieftains' edifice complex.
Icons of commerce. European churches. Sired
from the lineage of post modern Medicis:
GE, AT&T, RCA, PANAM, SEARS.

Sophia D. Etxeberria

Clustered in concentric circles - - straight square,
right angle, trapezoidal distinction. Stone clad.
But structures decay, images fade, irritate
the eye. Casual remarks are made concerning "higher order."
Like old wives, monuments are tossed out, in search of
"cheaper space,"
in Jersey, with simple designs.
Queens are given bouquets by aficionados
of post modern architecture, others are
demoted
to ghettos. Diminutive new brides, with arched entries, burst
up in the Grand Openings, entertaining personal reviews in the
New York Times. Beneath this ganglia of tangled foundations
lies a nation of land memories: wild rose, cat tails, sweet sage,
annihilated by greed and a lack of clarity, with studied
indifference.

Forget winter

In winter I think of summer.
In summer I cannot forget winter.
I want you to slap me. Give me pain.
It is better than feeling dead.
Sex and death, lost in my pocket
like money - - killing time.

The night is quiet. Kiss me.
The candle burns. Wake me.
We dream and make love
and dream of making love.
There is power in destroying.
What are we waiting for?

Take me. Not a word. You are late
without calling. I hate you
and fear for my safety beneath
your surface, but I slide into
your lap, giving no warning.
For certain, you are well mannered.

Sophia D. Etxeberria

Breakfast in Jackson

It's your faults that make me
love you, the way you unabashedly
enslave me, your obsession with pain,
the way you sleep on the floor, naked
and pale as I stab my heart into you.

This river is death. This arrogance,
this manipulative word "courage."
The soft wing of day whispers with
danger as we fall in shades of yellow,
deep yellow. Cold, quiet yellow. Only
the blue sky could conquer you.

You think of me in passing,
like a song. It is your want
of love that brings the wind,
and your swollen sorrow.
The deformed seduction of death
has mingled with your unwept soul.

Jokaldi

How can I tell this story
of all the things that went wrong?
How can I ever sing about
this long, slow pain?
I know you will not forgive me,
but I meant no harm.
This pain, it makes you bitter,
it just takes its time.

Last night you called me godless.
I was certain you did not love me.
I lay awake thinking
how little you know me.
You think you know someone
when you know their crimes.
When I awoke you were kissing me
and Easter bells were ringing.

Some things are so dangerous
you have to steal them like a song
who becomes the voice who sings it,
like a heart that has been broken
and then learned to forget,
like a fool who cannot be cured
of his love for the dance.

Sophia D. Etxeberria

Gold

This voice was torn from the wind and sent to you.
It was captured in the forest by sun rising through dew.

The din of the sun rising is the terror of the human soul
banished long ago to the mountains of Peru.

Extravagant explosion of flowering orange, beat of zebra,
pace of time, so easy to misconstrue.

They fly on the wind in a velvet hum,
hummingbird wings of green and blue.

Good men serve women and good women serve men.
The pounding sun lives in us. It makes this world true.

Esposo

His breath releases in the middle
of sleep. It is a sigh.
Not hopeless. Not discouraged.
It's like the way he says our children's
names. You can hear the sadness
if you listen closely.
He says we'll be alright.
"There is nothing you can do
to keep them from leaving."

He rarely tells me I'm beautiful
but he knows how to hate me. He cringes
at the wickedness, pulls the covers
up to his chin, lays very still
when I come slithering back
as if I were a rattler
unable to stay away from his heat,
his starry dream-filled eyes.
He can dream just as fast as me,
he can chase the nightmares away.
He doesn't run from pain.
But he swears he'll kick the shit
out of the next man that messes
with me. He always wants to
know names, dates, and places.

Sophia D. Etxeberria

One August he picked sage
broke it under my nose
rubbed it over his hands and jeans,
promised to paint the house,
chop firewood, clean the gutters,
but.. . and ...
he begs me not to read my poetry
for fear of nightmares.
He says I love my dog more,
that I would have to choose between
them and him. I said I'd love whomever
I wanted. He stayed.

Last Thursday he woke me early
to make his coffee. I caught his reflection
in the window from the far
end of the kitchen. He was
petting my dog. Looking at me. Waiting
for coffee. I love my husband
and I love my dog (whom I can live without)
That is the difference between the two
and everything else I'm about.

Heat

Today the only thing that moves
is the heat. It undulates over
us all like a demanding lover. I watch.
No one sees me. Everyone's eyes
are shut in concentration.
The heat is heavy.

If you were here would you see
me? I walk to the corner thinking
of you. I walk back. My heart is
swollen. I try to breathe one truth
but the air won't move.

Last night I was afraid. Do I have
what it takes? Today I am lonely.
Where are you? The heat undulates
over us all as if it is superior.
I need one well established truth
to break this dogmatic heat wave.

Sophia D. Etxeberria

Break Point

My father died when I was eleven
in a snow storm in Kansas. That
was the end, not of innocence
(for I do not believe in the concept
of lost innocence) but of silence.

Now my mind is haunted
with songs like roads that lead me
back to that break point, that fissure,
that space that opened in my heart.

A broken heart exists beneath me
and in everything I do. Like a river
that gradually disappears from sight,
it flows far below my surface
to some unknown destination.

Tradition of evening

Life slows on land
not far from tradition.
Simple matters of virtue
still blossom from milky
violet skies. A faint world
of the clean and pristine
resonates from the tip
of the stem of an apple,
calls for a returning
to space.

Wolf spider weaves
the web of retrieval.
In her home resides
an accumulation of decay.
Slopes and shadows smudge
leaves and legs of insects.
She is the middle distance
between unobscured pain
and the thawing of the wind:
A sound that cannot be taught.

Sophia D. Etxeberria

We sleep in the way we live.
Minds and imaginations lure
cacophonies of color.
There is no time anymore.
No new element.
Tradition flows from land,
from an unfazed sky
of impenetrable scent.

A wife works quietly nearby,
turns her hands
in the soft plum
of evening, blends
the profane and the sacred
into one.

Pain

Stay away
the air is cold
your wife and child wait
yawning in the sunlight
far from despair, while
the death of us is near.

I stare at the stars
they carry my memories
like a river echoes
like caves and tombs
of men with common sense

Don't call me back
the sky is open
your horse is strong
and I dry my own pain
because this is my
way of serving you.

Sophia D. Etxeberria

September

Let's sail to heaven like this. Launched
far from home with our legs and arms fitted
together like the planks of a boat, the soles
of our feet nestled perfectly to form
a stern. Let's float, taking time with us,
the stars above, and the sea below.
Let's wrap ourselves in a cool metallic
warp of breathing, gathering in the dusk.

All we are borne from, the land, our blood,
our pain, all that is a wall now, an impenetrable
fortress from where the wind swells and pushes
us further and further from the shore. Let's dangle
our fingers in the sea, letting our hands
leave a wake of dreams in everything behind us.

Petradom weather

Perched on the bow,
smashing through angry gray sea.
Icy water rains down.
Petradom weather.
Black specks in the sky - - visions,
flying in arching patterns,
desperately scan the clouds,
pitch out across the horizon,
disappear far from shore,
soaked with ocean spray.

It counts:
this fruitless search in
streaked shearwater off
a remote island in the Aleutians,
where a skua, blown to U.S. soil
while migrating to Siberia,
excretes salty brine
from his nostrils like
a man in his first confession
of fallibility in being a man.

Sophia D. Etxeberria

Our boat devours the wind,
dips in and out of waves and
troughs at high speed. Glides.
Leaps. Torpedoes the surface
like a dolphin skipping across
sterile deep waters saving
us from the inertia question:
Are we part of the infinite,
the Pink-orange dawn tints
of the Arctic Circle flowing over tundra?

Glaciers smear off tops of diamond pipes,
spread tiny yellow, purple, green
pebbles westward. And all the while
I am trying to land in rain,
snow, and darkness. Unnerved
by anger, careening into the trivial
night amid a litany of problems
and distractions
having to do with my love life
and what I ate for breakfast.

Smoke of dusk

A little motor manages to sputter
and cough a couple of hours each evening
before nightfall lets down like a woman
clean and sprawling in the dark.
The water heater will not run.
We drenched 2400 ewes in three days.
No bath for 2 weeks.
It is difficult to get much reading done.
The picture of the children
in the river blurs
in the cold smoke of dusk.
Stars scuff the bare horizon,
rise like sparks above the pebbles
in the road back to Huancayo.
I have packed the two trunks
with 20 alpaca rugs,
fox hides, pinto sheep hides,
and the huacos.
Now, at night, I think
of three things:
250 replacement ewes
missing from the spring of '56,
my regret of leaving pilots
training in '45,
and just before sleep, Abanto
slashing open bags of DDT.
His knife, I vaguely recall,
is where my death began,
where your soul learned to speak.

Sophia D. Etxeberria

Ghost Dance

My father was buried in a pit
of ancient, fecal slime.
He crawled out last night to
the edge of my dream and
asked me to change
his black to snow.

My father drifts in a sky
with not one solitary cloud
only a condor flying
and an insect drinking
from a pine needle
Sunday morning dew.

My father rode a dark mare.
He came back for his maroon handkerchief and paisley tie.
I chased his ghost into the corn
field. "Go on home!" I yelled.
He did not look back.

The long good-bye

For as long a she knew him
he'd been saying,
"I'm going to die."

She cried at night and
every time
he was late.

She tried to hide things in his
food, dirt clods
Chilean sky.

One day she said, "So be it.
It is after all
your life."

People were very shocked when
she ran off with
a Mexican waiter.

He wore pointy black shoes.
"Blood Honkey,"
they whispered.

Sophia D. Etxeberria

Mr. Sever's Trees

Trees are not so discontent:
The wind blows their leaves
to perforate the neutral sky.
Yes, branches rearranging clouds,
but in their defense, they also
overlap to create shadows
for dogs to lie down to rest
and for squirrels to bury
treasures and not forget.

There was a rear view mirror
that captured this spell: The
leaves and wind in a neutral
sky and a man driving by.
A woman's face lit by Pluto
and a street lamp. She was
digging like a dog searching
for a bone or a Catholic Pagan
making herself at home.

The Circus
(after reading The Garden, by Ezra Pound)

Like a tusk of a wild boar thrust into the night
He stands on a platform high above the Moscow Circus,

And he is living off bits and pieces of adrenaline.
And below there is a rumble
Of the hard working class, sound-sleepers of the very content.
They will keep this country running.

In him is the beginning of danger.
His tension is practiced and protracted.
He waits for someone to fall to him,
And is almost certain I will be the one
              To leap in his direction.

Sophia D. Etxeberria

Adios

All I have are these letters.
You are gone
gone like last year

All the love and advice
I will ever receive
from you, written
on fifty three pages

Life is disappointing but
you would have been the
last to sit around and brood
about what has taken place

I take your words
mix them with my own
but you are gone
gone like last year
and every year before.

X

Are you hungry? Because
you make me nervous.
I dreamed of you ripe
and swollen like plums.
To say you carry the scent
of harvest, or the fecund
dirt of the river bank
is to speak only of your
flavor, for you exhale
the opium of prayers,
prayers rising to heaven
from saints in love
with humanity, falling
to their knees the way
I fall to you, inhaling
strange traces of man.

Sophia D. Etxeberria

Samba

Desire, like fallen
snow, the legacy
of water, or secrets
of night, struggles
just as surely as the
black dog paces on
his rope to nowhere
as the indignant majority
floats through heat
above the flame.
Hope for desire to strike,
strike everywhere,
in the touch
of the baker's hand,
in rhythm of the
Samba, sweet samba
mother's milk of
lovers everywhere.

On the eve of destruction

In your arms, I could be destroyed.
In your warm flesh,
muscles tight,
I could lose this life,
this steady, calm peace
in your arms, your eyes, your lips
bitten blue.

I've lost it before, from playing the violin too young, all of those moods carousing through my innocent veins.

I play my eyes, my words, my smile
for you,
because in your arms,
I know, I know
I could be destroyed.
Look. Look at me.
Me, in your arms,

sanctuary from your steady,
calm peace. "...Madness and more
of Sin...the soul of the plot."
Says Edgar Allen Poe.

Sophia D. Etxeberria

The storm

Camouflaged by leaves
and the sound of water
falling off the edge
rippling out to touch
the hidden ache of souls
drifting,

They avoided the
electric rapture
of spirits flying the wind
on a cloudy day
when everyone was praying
for relief.

Power lines sizzled,
hit by dry white
lightening.
Sirens screamed.
Dogs howled.
Fingernails pierced
the flesh of sin.

A serious chat

In this room,
room of man and woman,
room of divisions,
there is a polarity between
boldness and compassion,
passion and caution,
the innocent,
and the dammed.

Here.
Take my cigarette.
Smoke it.
Breathe it.
It is my gift to you.

Sophia D. Etxeberria

Date at the carnival by the sea

What to wear:
Cotton candy panties
Tilt-A-Whirl bra, Coke-a-Cola
lipstick, with a splash
of taffy at the cheek. Roller Coaster hair
tied up with a licorice rope.
Essence of popcorn.

B.B. Gun tights. Kamikaze Boots.
Twister skirt, guaranteed
to make a man scream all the way down
the Zipper. Thing-a-ma-jigs dangling
from lobes. Hot pretzel behind
one ear. Haunted House sweater filled
to maximum occupancy.

The Date:
You took one look, called me Sky-Ride,
blew five dollars in my arcade.
In the Casino, Wild Cat thighs
pressed tight. Side Winder arms
tangled in a snake dance.

Sustenance

In a mirror, dusty dim,
cracked in the upper corner
from a red high heel
flung in a rage,
she touches her breasts
and thinks of the mouths
that suckled her
nipples.

Hungry mouths of young
men in dark, cramped rooms,
or in corn fields under
summer solstice sky.
One drowned in
the river, another
shot himself in
the head.

The greedy one from Spain
bit her twice as two men
stood by, watching,
looking down,
hard and cold.
Hatred grew in
that wound, but
not forever.

Sophia D. Etxeberria

There were infant mouths,
passed back and forth,
among sisters, sucking
mothers' milk.
Those mouths grew.
One sang an Irish ballads
at a bar in a
diaphanous dress.

She had a hungry
lover who pretended
to be hungry.
Shy and quiet,
as she unbuttoned
her blouse. The Whole
thing was
counterfeit.

Captain Logan's Paradox

The lonely man steps out to the night.
All around, moonlight has frozen to molecules
that breathe his quiet, still thoughts of love.
In the cold air full of shadows,
his lungs, fragile with madness,
shrink from contact, evading
a silent matter of desperation.

Time, the inaccessible enemy, pulsates
and ignites a flame in his soul,
alive with the small hope of an innocent.
Past the streets and dark alleys, past
sheer cliffs and wild crags, beyond
his shyness, he longs to be kissed.

The great hymns of the church arise full
of promise, but when night dissolves
the language of day, he searches,
once more, for someone to wonder
where he is, someone with warm
arms who will stir him into remembering
some little line from this gigantic poem.

Sophia D. Etxeberria

Justo y la luna en el río de La Plata

The moon has risen from the black river tonight
to glaze the surface with silver light.
I cannot think of how to comfort you,
or myself, or anyone else. It has shattered
the waves like an electrical current
zig-zagging through cracks of water.

I am mute like an animal with no explanation,
blinded by the shimmering reflection
scattered before me. Like a poor, dumb
burro I bray, "The moon is in the sky!
The moon is in the water!" Our boat
speeds faster, faster.

Light splits and bounces. It skips across
the black mirror, makes itself a part of every
drop, spraying from the stern as we fly
beneath the sky. You laugh. I feel your eyes
move up my legs. Sliding beneath my dress.

Like a sail I open myself to the wind,
the night air, to every question. I could
untie myself right now and dive into the water.
I could untie my hair, the white scarf around
my neck, and all civility. And I do. White
spills from my hands. It falls silently, effortlessly.
I cannot explain this to you, or myself, or anyone else.

Time has cut my tongue the way silk cuts a river.

Jackpot Nevada

Across the silence of the desert
voices bleat through white light
and dust, calling for their mothers.
And the scent of sage opens
like a pink rose, spreads to the shadow
temples of dawn, sullen, golden,
finding broken hearts scattered in shards
of violet, as violet as butterfly wings.

They drop to the Earth, empty men,
ashamed, unable to connect, they weep.
The women drape themselves over their
backs like great birds, spreading
their wings, holding the men's hands,
joining their fingers in perfect circles
as they breathe and pray. Their children
kneel all around them. The world
prepares for war. And everything
shivers like leaves awaiting rain.

Sophia D. Etxeberria

The name game

The Fun House man ate our tickets,
guessed my perfume: Waves Breaking.
In the Hall of Mirrors, I became
Lady Sea Dragon with the amazing
shrinking head, Bumper Car buttocks.
You were Mr. Burrito Underwear.
Hot dog ears. Shooting star.

You wanted to ride the Holland Express
to a Nebraska rain storm.
We rode until the clouds burst,
soaked in reflected lights,
drenched by garish dawn,
locked beneath safety bars.
High speed, backwards, forwards.
Minds in a dream river,
flowing from cranium to cranium
while two girls behind us
screamed Godddddd!

The mathematician's cave

There are words in my heart with no place to go:
gardenias opening to rain, butterflies crushed by snow.

I want to sing like the ocean. I want to be brave,
to swim beneath the sun in the liquid warmth of a shoal.

When you ride on the wind look back to the sea.
Breathe. Breathe. Be willing to console.

I am kneeling. I am naked. I am opening to rain.
For the rain of Las Marismas rules my soul.

Two goldfinch eggs, a gift for you I can't explain.
Take them to your world. Find the pulse. Behold.

Sophia D. Etxeberria

Hologram

We split apart and come together as easily as rain,
our enfolding and unfolding cannot be explained.

We met on the ocean when our fathers looked away,
our mouths were as human and as certain as pain.

Separated by fantastic and ordinary illusions
your hand on my thigh is only the physical plane.

Look again. It is all walking towards us.
What keeps us from touching is simply the profane.

The wind compels us to lift our hearts to the sky,
to laugh and sing only about what remains.

What a woman wants

In conversations about what men and women
want, there is no third person. There is only
you and me. Whatever bruises of the flesh
have been left, all now depends on whether or
not we are willing to do this one thing supremely
well, to let love do what it once did for all of us.

Intrepid men are still about, readers and dreamers
who guard the past when much of the rest of the
earth lies in ruin. They astound me, holding on
to their faith, standing alone in nature, devoted to
noble goals. Any one of them who wants to feed
me, I'm quite willing to accept their blessings.
And if it should ever be in the morning, let
it be with blackberries and cream.

But if it should ever be at night (did you
see the full moon?) let it be with curiosity.
And if I suggest we proceed with haphazard
panache, and then interrupt with a knife
at your throat, turn your face toward mine.
Hold steady. See and take all of me.

Surely, Umberto, lack of spontaneity
is the greatest deprivation. For we are far
more than Basque monarchs. We are Sherpas
choosing our own paths. If we should ever meet
again, be certain enough to take away my
knife. Be swift enough to give me poetry.

Sophia D. Etxeberria

To my brother at sea

I am jealous of time, the way
it widens out over the Atlantic
deep with endings and beginnings,
navigating like a ship
with canvas sails unfurled
over your light-weight caravel.

Tonight the Black Coast of sorrow
is dressed in blue and the silken
breath of the Azores shudders beneath
the length of becalmed days. On the surface
stars are reflected like silver clouds
of swallows. And beneath the depth
of the sky, swims the nature of man.

Time has seduced you to the sea.
The salt air has converted
the roundness of your world to
a sailor's horizon, distant like the shore,
or the clamor of bells in the wind
or the names of the Great Khans
of Karakorum. You stand watch,
fastened to the deck by an invisible
string of intricate knots.

Sing me the Southern Song, your gentle
lullaby, low and graceful. Sing in your
lonely way of singing like an Egyptian bird.
I will listen for you in the ache
of the chestnut trees, the cathedral
of St. Sophia, in the origin of words,
calculating the time-speed distance
equation when we will meet again.

Argentina

Men like to be squeezed by strong thighs as if they
would never be let go,
and they never get over this because we never
get over anything.

Even now my blood runs black with the things of women.
Everywhere I go, whatever I do, there it is: Sun sleeping
in your hair, music rising from a mandolin in Mendoza,
tangos of crowded barrios in Buenos Aires.
And all the while I am longing for
light falling through the mist
just beyond the path
of tipa trees.

You lie there at the majestic, fully clothed, murderous, wild.
The horses sound
so pleasant trotting past the hotel window, horses with buggies,
horses with wagons. It is impossible to recall when this began.
You say
it came across the Andes in the middle of summer, snow
falling. Across the pampas in outdated railroad coaches.
From Lima. From southern Patagonia. From
the Hotel Cosmos in Punta Arenas. You voice scours like
wind. I press
my hands
to my eyes all the while longing for red
bougainvillea entwined with columns
of cold stone like lovers,
hand in hand, arms
embracing necks,
kissing.

Sophia D. Etxeberria

Around 5:30 couples emerge from teahouses, matinees, or elegant shops,
gracefully stroll across green, rolling lawns, passing the time.
Somewhere
after 8:30, after an excellent dinner with Dr. Heine, after palm, cedar,
olive and pine segue to night, after 'loneliness struggles through the uncertainty of romance, we fall to the mercy of thighs.
Fall to the point-blank hazard of wanting love.
We never get over this because we never get over anything.
But all the while
I am longing
for you.

Happy birthday baby

Blue water tastes like drops
of sky, like the wind served '
at the Ferris Hotel in Rawlins, Wyoming.
Actually, I can never tell if it is wind,
or just the shadow of leaves shifting.
It doesn't really matter:
Everything explodes eventually.

We live in a very sexy world.
Everything pounding the air, the soil,
the skyline painted horizon.
This thing pollinates that.
Up-thrusts everywhere you turn.
Gaping holes being filled, especially
at the gas stations. Whew!
Lovers roll over and sleep
in long winter orgasms
as if touch was the most everlasting
state of grace on a planet
bursting with bombs.
Even the frog cries out,
"No! Not yet! Just one second more!"

Oh. Did you confuse the sexual void
with the gaping hole of death?
Frozen eyes, stiffened limbs, silent cries?
No. Dying is a solid state-fixed, ripe.
Bones tell the stories: bad birth,
slow hopelessness. Bloated excess.

Sophia D. Etxeberria

Try to remember: if you see something
with legs sticking straight up in the air,
this is not The Tao of Sex
calcified in an objective moment.
This is simply food for the magpie.

Flamenco

A man calls to a woman from the Celtic rain.
He calls with the rhythm of India.
He calls in the heat of the Moorish breeze
and she answers:

"Sweet as almonds and honey."

We dance because we are ancient.
We sing because we are borne.
In flamenco we have found a way
to move closer to the romance of God.

Sophia D. Etxeberria

Bengal tea

In an afternoon of Bengal
tea, Chopin rain,
cinnamon coffee cake
baking in General Electric.
She remembered you

your face turned
to the stars, searching
the night, the dark
shadow of salvation
for your breath.

You were holding her
like a mother,
like a father
eyes ready to weep.
"Sleep on my chest.

Leave it alone," until
tomorrow, when it
will screech
back in the light
of ordinary day.

Saratoga

Dreams are skipper stones that sink to the bottom of a lake.
Their roundness spins around like the roundness of heartbreak.

Today I am a stone spinning beneath the Wyoming sky.
Clouds drift above; white turtle, white seahorse, white drake.

Lie down by my side. Lay down your heart. Lay down your dreams.
Let the wind and water sing. Let them keep us awake.

What shall we be today? Which man? Which woman?
I'll be the sky and you ride the mare at daybreak.

You be the man taking off your brown leather boots.
I'll swim beneath your surface, a smooth, elegant snake.

Gernika

In time everything will be taken from me.
Like the Orio, I will give myself up to the sea.

One season will unwind into the next,
green velvet will spill into winter's ebony.

But for now, light spreads across your bed
as I rise to dress and pour your tea.

Before our memories dissolve into midnight,
before silence takes hold and reduces us to humility,

let us stand at the edge of this Earth wound
and fall apart in a fine, spinning melody.

Tumpa

Like a peasant, I am bound
to the land for survival. God will not
save me from the cruelty of nature
or from myself. Wind and darkness change
to trouble just as surely as I turn away
from my small idea of love, just as surely
as your heart beats long into the night,
as surely as your tears
will be my words.
      Now, I have kissed no one but you.
      Pancho Anduago thinks I should have taken
      the luscious 21-year-old at the elegant ball in Piura.
      Drowning in the clean smell of soap,
      incited by the manners of the Americano,
      the balm of her voice
      was rivaled in loveliness only by
      our children's laughter.
      I found myself turning away
      so disillusioned with living in Peru.
      By now she has retuned home to silence,
      her mind filled with more than dreams,
      for dreams have a habit of flying off
      just as soon as they have landed.
Night before last, too foggy to think,
I let my little mind wander home,
past the chunchos of the Amazon,
past the monkeys and the jackals,
past the two prostitutes offered by a man
as if they were a drink.

Sophia D. Etxeberria

Beneath Kachina Bridge. Between the Moenkopi,
Chinle, and Wingate formations, desert
and silver sky converged in a stream.
And each drop fell a thousand times over,
trapped in sandstone,
an echoing waterfall.
        It is after dinner, quite late. Tumpa
        grumbles beneath the Earth. The windows
        are filled with Inca rain. In the morning
        I go to Cajamarca to visit a fellow's puna.
        then to the market place to procure
        The 7x64 Czechoslovakian rifle
        I mentioned for 3000 soles.
        I work for the day I will see you again,
        and for grace, the essence of all my prayers.

Remembering Jesus and the last supper of my father

I am the face of a woman
who longs for the fragile,
shy kiss of your eye,
Venezuela blue, palm trees, oranges,
the sweetness of your breath
in a dark room, and your language.

I don't speak your boy name, Domingo from the stars,
shoved into the pit of an outhouse,
dangling upside down, breathing the shit
and piss of your family
as your mother's knife screamed
at you in Spanish. Sacrilege.
Sacrilege.

As a father, you swung me into the air
and commanded me to look, to envision,
to capture again and again the sheen
of the crow's nocturnal wing,
but all I've ever found in crow feathers
is the shadowed breath of your flight
and the blackness of your hair.
Now all your colors elude me.

Pobre mi corazon.
"Busco en mi pecho la calma, sueño de mi alma,
de mi corazon". How I wish you were here.
Weren't you the one who died
so far from home?
So many wounded phantoms.

Sophia D. Etxeberria

I watched you step from the edge,
lured by jagged, painted dancers
shaking their palo de lluvia,
beating los bombos. Ah, how translucent your skin.
You were laughing, drunk on pisco, naked in their arms.
It's nothing you said. It's only the wind,
and I believed you: your gossamer white blew
further and further away
until I could no longer hear the sound
of you in my mother.
God how she's hated you.
I thought I saw you in a man's eyes yesterday
filled with South American oranges and waves of palm trees
splashing life all over me.
I had to look again and again.
I barely know him and I've hardly any courage
since you went away,
but I wept beneath his magnificent sky.
If we could touch,
I'd promise to be content, again.

I long for crow feathers,
orange rinds, coffee,
for your face in my dreams.
Mingo, if you are in hell,
Jesus is there, too,
protecting you.

Tierra de mi padre

The night weeps into the open sea
deep sea, warm foam and froth
touching anything that drags across this strange landscape

noli tanger, exhale
for the man gone adrift in a dream

I can hear his cry sinking down
rolling off the boat's gunwale
floating in plumes like clouds of sperm

It drifts somewhere tropical
dives into black notes
They are waiting. They are waiting.

Not until I stepped into the streets of Spain
did I see that all roads lead away

They have been where I have been
and where I am going
They were taking me away as you were leaving

Night falls on them, turning,
growing quieter and more secret
like tall fragrant grass, laguna de Magdalena

call the wind, grow at my side
plant your seed on this night of sadness

The hoot owl watches
He is waiting. He is waiting
for the things in you that I will never touch.

Sophia D. Etxeberria

Sunchabamba

There is an elegant fall when silk is unfastened by a man.
It is a whisper, an echo, a wave crashing on the sand.

Why does a man cast a shadow on his woman's skin,
shadow of myrrh, shadow of dust from a Persian caravan?

Red silk. Cloud silk. Iris petal and leaves. Take them.
Take them from her. Hold them in your hand.

When a woman turns aside she reveals the secret of her
throat.
Taste her salt. It comes from the blood. I think you
understand.

We are ancient. We are traveling, unfolding in other worlds.
We are spinning. We are falling in Bizkaia, Germania, and
Iran.

Excommunication

Beloved,

In the night of betrayal, I will offer my body and bloodsatiate your hunger with a burst of dark cherry dipped in the melting bitter sweet of always wanting more. On a stripped altar,
I will lay a leafless white lily at your feet, fill the barren tabernacle with your raw chalice, unprotected by bread, or wine,
or chocolate.

I will be a stained-glass window under an intolerable longing for rain, unveiled of innocence on a varnished pew carved from parched earth. I will dismantle your holy rail, slip the communion on my tongue-the Bavarian creme, the Swiss mocha
- nail you to a sexual cross with infinite, delectable bites.
And after, beneath an unclothed pulpit with no royal purple vestment, no Bible, no sacraments, we will lie naked in a crèche,
enveloped by stark incense, peeled raw in marble candlelight. Only then will I hear your confession. Only when you are exposed
in the all together before the Father, Son and Holy Ghost.

P.S. If you want to bring along a bag of Doritos and a bottle of Tequila, that will be okay, too.

Sophia D. Etxeberria

Zeru aingeru (heavenly angel)

Little wooden matches spark the heart's desire.
Little sisters lift their skirts to fan the fire.

The hips of a woman move with poetic ease,
between the hands of men they sway with desire.

Speak slowly. Speak your words. Whisper at my throat.
We are lovers, angels drinking from pools of sapphire.

A sorgin winds around a room like a trail of smoke.
Gamblers watch, dealers, a Taurus, and a soldier.

Zeru Aingeru, why do you follow me in such a dark way?
Every poem I send to you makes me more and more a liar.

Nothing more than this

Like the sea and the ship, we
drift through the night,
softly. My breath against
your back, your back against
my breath, rocking gently
against one another under
a glimmer of sky, with the breeze
in the curtains and our dreams,
fathoms deep beneath us.

You sigh, tired from labor,
it folds back like a wave,
breaking over and over. Like
the stars, you leave before dawn.
Like the stars, you return
at night. Now and then,
during the vast blue of day
1 think of us colliding
softly in moonlight.

Sophia D. Etxeberria

The measure of all things

Out of darkness your hand
cuts the wick, strikes the match,
lights the flame that stretches
with ease over Moroccan linen.

Your arms, relaxed and secure
like a sleeping fox behind
the crystal bowl of sour
black cherries, washed and cool.

Scattered night, flowing
from the table like time ,
speaks to our immediate need
for hot breath and sweet mouths,

the forgiving day, and lips
full of forgetfulness
and our child, still warm
and slick between my hips.

Alone

I have no prayers to churn
the river. Sun trapped
in cliffs of stone and light
terrifies me. The sound
of that enormous night,
when our bodies bound
in privacy and lovely
offerings found our secrets
slowly filling the air
with heavy murmuring whispers,
is locked out.

All here is silent, a sealed
tomb guarded by jackal headed
gods. But through the stillness,
traces of colored light,
smudges of pure gold,
fired out of descending, sinking,
hope, crawling on his
belly at the center of my heart.

Sophia D. Etxeberria

A rough idea

Faith comes...
    like a point of color amidst the shadows of fish,
   the way you look for someone to give you what you deserve.
    Everything.
    Or didn't deserve. Any of it.

The humans...
    gauge the road ahead with a compass set
    to the astronomy of cruelty or kindness.
    Even equality is a rule of measurement. Wild
    horses decipher the opposite: wind and water.

Long ago...
    we traded self governance for protection;
    fireflies in the woods for inalienable rights.
    Freedom to find what we have lost, is freedom
    to weep for what we have lost.

Trade...
    politics for more politics, still the wind rustles the trees.
    Some of this and that has already been taken care of,
    like sand and waves, not by students or science
    or even the honest politicians.

The wound...
    of faith comes like seeds
    hidden in a pumpkin field.
    I say wound, because faith is a knife
    that liberates the seeds.

Wind Rod

Saguaro
hear wind
chasing javelina
through cholla
tingling spines
catch it, hum
hurry run
hoot
of owl
responds.

Mantorni

Magic collapses beneath the weight of moon-glow.
It sweeps the wind with dragonfly wings of indigo.

Take back your life from the Tibetan Book of the Dead.
Lift it from pages captured long ago.

Forget the Mantorni, the one who broke your heart.
She is part of you now, a lovely scar, a memento.

The warmth of night is full of sounds and wounds.
Swim in its darkness. Float in the sound of embryo.

I am coming to you. I am walking. I am riding a horse.
I am singing a lullaby. I am waiting in a shadow.

In another language

Our words slide
around each other
with lips pressed
like rose petals
between pages
written in the language
of kissing.

Vibrations
smoke my senses,
slash the dark
like sunlight split
by Venetian blinds
in a hot room
on a summer afternoon.
My voice echoes back,
lover, timeless, more.

Entwined, your mouth
at my breast,
scent of hair,
sweet breath,
sweat,
hot liquid silver
on my tongue,
belly, thighs
burns a trail of sighs
to the stars.

Sophia D. Etxeberria

The shore

I carry you with me, out
the door, with my hairbrush
in my purse, walking along
the boardwalk with the coast
before me and the sea grass
and the wind and the sky
leaning into me like morning,
arms around my waist,
thick with Florida heat.

I walk with the bruise
beneath my lip while you sleep,
arms stretched above your head
like a sailor pulling ropes
of air and light with ease.
I make love to your face
tangled in my hair, crushed
into the surface of my skin
like salt: strong and exquisite.
So sad. So deep. So clean.

Paco de Lucia

The Spaniards stand in the street,
city suits pressed and clean.
American women in high shoes,
laugh, exhale cigarettes and garlic.

They inhale exhaust from the street,
lace and silk brush against
sweat and cologne.
The city exhales.

Street lights, car lights,
erect and bright lights
theater lights. Breathing,
the women wait

for flamenco stars, intrigue,
private lessons, and the cante.
The poetry of Paco' s guitar
has softened their hard mouths.

Sophia D. Etxeberria

Melody of Cordoba

You walk by
with your guitar
and songs, hungry
for the jasmine
in my hair with all
of Cordova taking
her evening stroll.
In the twilight,
eyes full of velvet
shadows and an old
woman selling figs
from a basket. You
take one, bite down
hard. I wonder
about the sweetness
of sun dried fruit
and what you might do
to please a woman you love.

Touch the body

"And I will restore to you the years that the locust hath eaten…"
Joel, 2:25

How strange that we could have learned
to mistrust kindness. Your hands touch
my face, slide across the lines,
ease pressure, tension, yours and mine.
They spread over my thighs like lava
coaxing smoke through my veins, intently
examining the muscles of a dancer's life.

I know you touch other women.
Do you shake when you breathe?
Forget to answer?
Does the sole of a foot reveal more than
a woman's hips? Does a pulse of a wrist
indicate a question? Is it an answer
if they do not resist?

In Italy and Greece you worked
in the vineyards. In San Francisco
you fried rice. Now you harvest roses
for oil. Touch the body. Touch the dirt.
Your whole life runs through your fingers,
is shaped and molded and absorbed
through the palms of your hands.

Sophia D. Etxeberria

Ramon

You have fallen into my soul
like a dog into an abandoned well
and I don't know how to save you
though you weep like a train
from deep within the night.

I come back to you, like the moon,
like the tide, the way red
leaves fall to the earth,
the way sails catch the windbecause
I have to.

The night, the stars, dreams,
they pass by your velvet doorway.
I don't tell them how to find you.
They call your name.
The wind and rain whisk it away.

Your hands have built a fire
in this place no one has touched.
I won't save you.
I don't thank you.
And still you call me back to life.

Señor Barrutia's reply

I could seduce you.
I would not shame you.
I might trick you.
I have no need
      to impress you.
I would not poison you.
I have no interest in defeating you.
Full passion only exists in our dreams.
I earn
sex as an interesting pleasure.
      Merlot or espresso?

Sophia D. Etxeberria

Guardian of night

Under the blessing of night
where moonlight gazes from fallen
snow and all the songs of the dead
await us, you lay your broken heart
beneath your pillow and rest beside
me, your face in my hand, forgetful
in sleep where the wild bird sings
by the river and flies to your
dream like a sigh. It is late. The sheets
are warm and my razor sharp blade
hides from the moon beneath the mattress.

Snow falls to the cold river. A car sputters
through slush, and the wind, wary of trees,
prays on the shore of the lake. Starlight
burrows into the rabbit's hole. Fire dies
to mute white ash. My sister, sweet in song,
and my mother's hand, guide me to sleep
where the night waits like a servant, watching
through gray eyes: bending to my face,
tracing my skin nestled against bone,
pulling me in with one hand in my hair,
the other, searching for the knife.

Piña de agave

Men and women come together,
souls in dreams, lonely guardians,
black swans who touch
in smooth, succulent light.
The shoemakers, the jewelry makers,
the distillers, they reach
for one another like lilies
in the rain, blanco, silver,
abandoning cavernous hearts
for a kiss.

There goes one now, her head
tucked down, shy and lovely,
reposado. The men come
from darkened fronts, the dusty
expanse. They taste of salt
and bitterness. She walks by
quietly thinking of love.
They drink her like sweet tequila.
She sees only the straight-neat
lines of the street. But their
breath is strong and fearless,
brushing the hair from her eyes,
guiding her like a hand
on the small of her back,
murmuring at her ear.
She arches her neck,
listening.

Sophia D. Etxeberria

Toro bravo

The ganaderos raise their bulls to move with ease and speed,
to charge the cape of the matador, not to concede.

The spirit of fight is inherited. The cow determines the bull.
At dusk horsemen ride to gather eight heifers to breed.

In the corral, magenta and yellow swirls round and round.
One heifer cuts back, charges, fights to be freed.

A mysterious thunderbolt flashes across the arena.
Dust and darkness enfold her, a ghostly, feminine creed.

The cape is ripped from the matador's hand. Birds let out a cry.
Extremadura torches flare. "This one will take the seed."

Snap and break

The waitress in the Golden Spike,
(false of tooth), the drunk who buys
us ice cream, the hag fish in the Rawlins Laundromat
who screams, "Shut up, brat! You want me to smack your face?"
They all know their parts. They've memorized their lines:
Check dryer for small children and pets before inserting
twenty-five cents. (It was a scary Laundromat.) Push to start.

But you've turned mean. You' re driving a big, red truck now.
You throw me forty dollars to pay for supper
while you make calls. Peeing out beneath Wyoming stars
in red cowboy boots and a nightshirt, I swear to you
I don't remember their names.

But see how their light reflects dimly in slick meadow grass.
And while we are on the subject, wood smoke does smell
like coffee, pine tar, damp lamb's wool, garlic,
like a waning moon, candle light, like your breath,
your sweat, and the soft soles of your feet.

The good mother hill still guards
the ranch house, looms beneath northern lights.
I know. I know. In daylight she's two hills,
one breast smaller than the other. Her aspen
leaves pitter patter in the sun. Pitter patter.
Flying ant, caterpillar, too, flash orange black.
Orange black. Wind tangles, harangues
sage brush. Whistle and scrape. Snap and break.

Sophia D. Etxeberria

Coyote patrol dens, hunt sheep.
Antelope chew. Deer watch.
Dogs guard sheep, and the sheepherder's horse
inches up and down the good mother hill,
around each and every sound
beneath the hum of the sun.

At night stars explode
all over her, except when clouds
block the light and lightening strikes.
Then, for one terrifying
second, everything between us
becomes electrifyingly clear.

Dreaming the Yellowstone
(for Trapper John)

The Yellowstone River flows toward you like the sex of men;
dream water slides through canyons, falls,
every drop completely unpredictable. Test the water.
Temptation begs you to complain.
Too much life. Cold enough to freeze a thought midstream.
Spills over lines, rules, safety rails. The edge laps at your feet,
gets everything wet.

Fed by rain, fed by tributaries, fed by snow, by springs high in
the Absaroka Range. Swift current. Patch of blue sky.
A mountain or two. Strip of stars overhead.
Shadow of a man. Shadow of a woman.
Sweet, sweet lupine, purple white. Horned toad, ant, badger
drinking from the bank.
They know about the slam of dreams,
lightening, wind, mood of every wave.

Shadow of a dog. Shadow of a boy.
Silt turns to mud beneath a double ended rainbow,
eyelid of God.
Superstition colored sky.
Feather in the willow. Shadow of a spirit.
Dreams are black onyx reservoirs.
Dreams are sweet, sweet lupine, purple white.
Dreams are stars riding the Yellowstone on a cold winter
night.

Sophia D. Etxeberria

Except for this

Late at night with twelve candles at my bedside,
and the light of the moon, my only friend in which to
confide,

who brought me to you and the wind, and the dusty road,
and the nighthawk calling from a high-flying glide.

I'm leaving. I'm going back to everything I once knew.
I'm taking you with me; I'm taking you as my guide.

There is nothing about you I understand. That is why you are
here.
I'm holding you. You are seeing me. Let the Virgin decide.

I know almost nothing, a few songs, a few dreams,
and that a butterfly unfolding is an invitation to ride.

Here comes misery

Your story has changed.
How romantic you've become,
opening the night with a brilliant
blue whistle, as sleep lays against you,
curled into your dreams, as soft
and strange as summer's end, spinning
in the cricket's song, nestled beneath
the wing of the dove, infused
with the aroma of leather. Like a diamond
winged wasp, you have found
your way to my bed.

I have no need for words, yet words
are all I have. You lay on my white
sheets, beautiful and dangerous. I
take your head in my hand and bend to
taste a late dinner of tangerines, trying
to make peace with your barbarism. The mercurial
slope of your hip intrigues my small, American
imagination. Taunts me. If I lay down
with you, somewhere in the night our souls
will twist and slide like the bellies of fish.
I have no courage. No courage.

Sophia D. Etxeberria

Shipwrecked

In the fourth hour I fell from the safety of the world
to faithfully await the dawn. I wasn't thinking
of you then. I was looking up. I was praying for
salvation. I was entering the mystery,
the private experience of the individual.

The sky turned high above the sea.
Every wave sighed in prayer. You
entered through the clear glass
window of the surface, coming to
me in rays of glittery groves beneath
the Sea of Cortes, casting long silhouettes
of dreams that lay beside my sunken ship,
smooth from centuries of use.

Once I lived in a time. Your mother had taken me
to see your room. I followed as if I had been called
to worship, cherishing the relics, inhaling the incense,
kissing the icons with my memory. But it was your bed
that guaranteed the safe deliverance of my soul, covered
in a quilt of gray doves, flying from a field of golden corn.

I want you to take off your religion, to throw
it behind the door, to stand behind me
naked, without fear, to meet me at the gentle
slope just above the inlet to the sea, to float
in this watery sphere where we will not act,
or sleep, or wonder, or cry out in any way
that is similar to your world.

Shanaz

There is no real reason why shades
of memories survive. Torn apart,
skewered from the souls of their making,
they return from hiding
in contingents,
separated, but never forgetting
where they come from.
One lately, so sensate
its fingers stick my heart,
keep me from peace, persuade
me to follow, over and over,
to saddle mi caballo de paso,
wrap my legs around Jarano,
to ride to the back of the house
where Lucho has been working
like mad to fix the plumbing.

He wears the 3 dollar shirt
I sold to Zunico
and a scarf. It is cool,
but not raining, and he
is not digging. A mandolin
rests on his shoulder,
presses against his cheek,
seduces his skin like a Persian
dancer. He speaks softly,
listens to her strings,
sings like water: "Ay que te quiero.
Ay que te quiero."

Sophia D. Etxeberria

The smoking lounge

I still smoke you like a thin cigarette. My doctor told me to sop. My husband says he'll leave if he catches me again. But when I'm alone, I curl up on the davenport, strike a match and wait for you to burn beneath my lips.
Smoke curls out to fill the smoking lounge with a wicked sent that follows me through the afternoon. I can wash my hands, take a shower, but I can't get you out of my mind, not yet anyway. I'm addicted to the slow burn.
When I drive I hold you low by the side window so there is no trace of you.
When I take you into my mouth, I turn my face so others won't know which brand I smoke. I let the red ash grow before I flick you to the wind, praying always that no forest fire will ignite. So far so good.
I sleep in this dream. This dream of you and me blowing in and out of each other, or burning, rolled together tightly in Drum paper. This winter when the ruby glow was set against a world of snow and ice, the only warmth I could find was thinking of you.
Did I tell you I want to die this way, with you on my lips? I want to blow you out in one last sigh before we are crushed beneath a pedestrian foot, flushed down a stool in an Argentinean restaurant. I want to feel my mouth, once more, open as if to kiss with my face close to yours, just before we touch, just before the smoke
stings my eyes.

Quiet the mind

In lonely midnight black rain
pours down, redeems heat,
crushes stinking, biting creatures
sliding through niches of arroyos.
Just beneath, aquifers have become
intimate with the sky. Dark water
flows below the Sonora.

Shadows slide across sandstone ravines
like wind gathering to kiss
the unsettling essence of orange trees.
Clouds spin soft sand of washes
into tingling dust devils.
A man's hands turn brown under the sun,
scratch Earth into submission.
Layers of sediment part to shelter roots
of saguaro or fig trees, or to caress
the dead and simple wisdom of a crucifix.

Quiet the mind. Listen to turtle singing
battle hymns to the morning star.
Listen to fog migrating inland.
Listen to horse pricking his ears, listening.
Listen to thunder explode in the heat.
Listen to priest buttoning his collar.
Listen to flash floods heading for the empty.
Listen to snakeweed slowly grow into a prayer.

Sophia D. Etxeberria

Death by chocolate

Slip it on my tongue.
Deep rum inflames
a burst of dark
erotic cherry beneath
melting bitter sweet.
And always
        wanting more.
Longing for rain
on parched earth
forbidden lips
or thighs pinioned by
        planets
is a nagging discontent
relieved only in
death by
        chocolate
Slip it on my tongue
Bavarian creme, Swiss mocha
        Godiva
Let me bare this sexual
Cross with infinite
Delectable bites.

Piura

Gusts of wind, in a sinuous
movement, smash the night's mask,
damage the solace of merciful blue
heave reassurance over the edge:
The biggest granja flood
since I have been here.

For two hours a roar and a lash
swept dark creases of hail and chaos
into seething pools of new water.
Then, countryside white and unformed.
Mesquite covering the land
in secret silver grace.
Narrow threads of vapor endlessly
intersected thinly sliced images.
The blood had drained away.
Wet and dark overlapped.
Small creeks turned to rivers
not even the horses could cross.

The storm caught up with me at Peña
Blanca. All the way home, air
enslaved by urgency and a swath
of plum. I crossed the stream by
the golpon. Layers of surface
dropped away, dangerously swept
by me, a tumultuous narrow
line between pain and ecstasy.

Sophia D. Etxeberria

Your face and the faces
of our children rushed by like stones
beneath the current, floated in
tentacles of bell clouds, long
and slender in a distant sky. Still
this mystic zeal lent no solace
to my simple loneliness.

Graywacke

If you were a wild horse
I'd name you Graywacke.
Paint your mane magnetite, azurite, volcano.
Splash your eyes turquoise sky.
Pound your hooves over hematite red beds.
Ride your back like a flying tree froggalloping,
galloping.

If you were a giant sea scorpion
I'd enlist Portuguese man-of-war
to surround you, hold you
captive in a Rugose coral reef
of Devonian waves lapping
so hypnotic only a dragonfly song
could persuade me to release you,
that, and your furious stinger.

If you were yellow I'd photosynthesize
the delicious, the capricious curve
of your mouth. I'd grow green, exhale
sweet oxygen, intoxicate winged insects
gently landing to pollinate, to copulate
on petals, leaves grown from listening to you.

Sophia D. Etxeberria

If you were a Luna moth colored
frosted mint and lilac,
studded with topaz and amethyst,
I'd dress in your velvet wings,
spin beneath Silurian stars
falling to us like rain,
falling to us like seed tufts
of a cottonwood tree.

If you were this dandelion, that earwig,
that precious opal, that black crow
I'd call you innocent, gift from God,
Earth-sky. I'd name you life.

Dobbertin

On a lovely ride to Peña Blanca
I saw a puma. Face to face
on a lovely road, the difference
between us so much greater than
anything you and I have squabbled over
with such disastrous results.

Unblinking. Unevenness. Suspicious signals
too immense to hold on to. Silence filled
the space between us, threatened to disorient me.
My elegant rifle stayed resting at my side.

In a slice of time he was gone.
Dust settled in a luminous halo
sweating in the sun and in the
clearing air four distinct images.

Deer, condensed in tight clusters
along the irrigated meadow ofla granja;
zorros on the verge of falling into deep space;
Pimentel shooting a lamb at 40 paces
for la cocina; and a signal, too weak
to be specifically detected
like light in an embryonic state.

Irretrievably lost to the morning breeze
they were nothing to hold on to
only a glimpse
of the subatomic interior.

Sophia D. Etxeberria

The light from your window

A universe of light in a drop of dew,
vibrating leaves of the forest, I send to you.

I was only ever a poet in love with the dawn
mesmerized by the silent wake of a swift canoe.

Mourning doves, sleepy soft light, a warm wind
they landed in my mind, and then away they flew.

The sorceress cast spells. The gardener plants seeds.
Why they spoke to me in algebra, I never knew.

The Lakota take their pain and turn it into prayers.
I take your eyes and try to see what is true.

Swimming in the hearts of saints

We are stronger in the presence of pure sound.
Mantras, sitars, screeching jaguars abound.

What name shall I call you? What fire shall I build?
A wall surrounds your heart, a fortress, a compound.

Visigoth, I inhale you like a black cigarette.
Listen. Can you hear the way my lungs pound?

We dance to become a part of every living song.
The giraffe hears us breathe as his feet touch the ground.

In the market place a man sings of love and fear,
Day and night his raga rhymes go round and round.

Sophia D. Etxeberria

A letter from the black virgin

It is difficult for me to name where things begin.
The train had passed in the night and switched tracks.
Men and women called out for one another. There
were cries and shouts. A man yelled to me. I did not
recognize his name. You quietly watched, a wild
heart searching for a place to spend the night.

You must have come from the broken sky,
arriving at my door, ravenous, boldly looking for love,
backing me down the hall to your room in the wake
of your cigarette smoke, the scent of your body
expanding in heat, my breath exhaling in a sweet
theater of consent. I felt as if I was twenty, although
I've never been twenty in all of my life.

The secret inhalation of your perfume revealed hidden
tricks: cruelty and laziness. The girl at the bar, the girl at the
table with the hands that floated in candlelight, the painted
girl, I could not calm her broken heart and so I reached for
 your face. My hands silently guided me to the tongue of
oblivion. You took your turn drowning me in the taste of
10,000 waves of confusion.

I thought you would come to find me at the cafe.
Every hour the bell tolled from the tower of the
Cathedral of Saint Francis, the origin of your reflection
became dimmer until I became a fearful rabbit in search
of a hole in which to hide. I'm waiting for you here,
waiting for you to dream us into the light.

Nietzsche is my boyfriend

For the longest time I have been scattered
in the strangest land among accidents
and things that were never my own.

Without relief, the spirits of every tree
in the forest whispered their poetry, shaping
and forming a thick parameter of questions.

Will I be loved? Am I innocent? Am I alone?
The past defied my comprehension:
the religions, the prayers, the sacred greatness.

The constant rush to escape resonated
through my world. Where ever shall I go?
What treachery will love ignite?

I wandered past small waterways, past
the human panorama, past the fires of
spiritual significance and into the open air.

Gradually I became at ease with the plodding,
slow pace and found myself in a region
full of billions of rocks,

split by a canyon of impossible proportions,
defined by a river where all gates swung
open when my boat touched the water.

It is this very word, I learned,
(impossible) that reveals the vastness
of my refuge. Now, there is no turning back.

Sophia D. Etxeberria

Impossibilities radiate all around me.
I have been swallowed to the middle
of a corkscrew. My heart is pierced.

Now I know my courage-loneliness.
I have found my danger-love of everything.
And so I have to leave you,

Because it has become so possible to kiss
your mouth, to kneel before you
in the safety of your little room ...

And Nietzsche won't let me see you anymore.

No! Nietzsche is my boyfriend!

Languishing at the edge of my pregnant thoughts
Oh, you are a cunning girl's name.
Bella, Isabella. How you have hurt me.
Let's go dancing! Once more!
Where Nietzsche will take us to the floor.

Sophia D. Etxeberria

Lullaby for a Buddhist monk

When a tree falls beneath the wave
of a broken-hearted man, there is
a thread of gold that shines up
to the sun looking for a place to
rest in the warm arms of a mother.

When a woman has painted everything
and there is nothing more to light, she
sits down to her sewing and pulls
on a lazy thread of silver until everything
in her reflection becomes her prisoner.

I am a woman and I know
what is being asked of me.
I know my part.
This is why I cannot
go to Cuba with you.

Father Ortiz

I suppose, now, you will confess me like a sin
to Father Ortiz at the Sacred Heart of Mary
this Saturday afternoon as if I were some terrible
and deliberate storm ripping through the night.

Lovers proceed from a practical sense of survival
and organized miracles-the start of everything.
There are other Gods, other words far beyond
their understanding. We can trust, though, that our
vocabulary makes us specifically human. It shatters
the first impulse, the original concept,
and all our private obsessions.

It is this language, stunned by a hot sky, that moves
us beyond permanent laments, frees us from staggering
images transmitted from Earth. This language,
in a deceptively direct way, contains
a dramatic element of movement, a dangerous
drive to become better and closer. This language,
an instinctive energy with a nuance of choice,
is not authentic.
It is effective.

Sophia D. Etxeberria

Father Ortiz goes grocery shopping

I suppose, now, you will organize
to free us from these staggering images
lamenting beneath a hot sky,
now t h at we have become dangerously instinctive,
closer to our authentic impulses,
each proceeding toward
our private concept of God.

Yes, Father Ortiz, your sin is transmitting
from the pulpit of the Sacred Heart of Mary
like a practical and direct language.
In other words, you are energetically shattering
the original concept of miracles, the dramatic
element of lovers to become closer,
to confess a terrible sense of survival.

It is this sense of survival that stuns us
into understanding that we are
specifically ripping through a nuance of Earthly
night, deliberately choosing
this human drive that we can trust
because just beyond our vocabulary
is the start of everything.

Father Ortiz at the car wash

Father Ortiz is down by the river.
He has become obsessed with images
transmitted from Earth. Stunned
by the nuance of lovers, he trusts
their private laments to become closer,
perceives this impulse
as the authentic vocabulary of God.

Mary's Sacred Heart believes
that sins are about as original
as Saturday afternoons,
and just as permanent. It is the miracles
that stagger through the first sky;
it is the dangerous miracles
that need to be confessed.

She is transmitting a dramatic language,
a direct lament that affects everything,
specifically lovers,
lovers who shatter the night with movement.
Their instinct for survival
rips through all concepts of organized deception.
Their vocabulary is dramatic and hot.
Their drive moves beyond the human element
to contain freedom.

Sophia D. Etxeberria

Father Ortiz in the office of the bishop

Let us proceed to the survival
of Father Ortiz who was never so much interested
in truth as the transformation of reality.
And, now, he has deliberately
become a terrible lover.

Father Ortiz has moved beyond sin.
He has dangerously staggered before the pulpit,
ripped through the confessional, and shattered
the deceptive concept of permanence.

We can trust, though, that Mary was originally hot.

Saturday sky.
Nuance of lovers.
Lament to be authentic.

And I want to say this before I have to go:

Night
Permanent
Shatter
Instinct.

Quepos

Sleeping through the dark
you rise and disappear
like green waves that undulate
before me in my dreams
pulling on my blood like the tides.

Naked, on the naked earth
we ask the moon to place
her faith in the palm of
our hands, rendered ghostly
by the shadowy light of love.

In a moment out of time
a falling, churning, froth of foam
and sand rush against each other
in dizzying attacks of swirls,
lines, coils. And I see.

My mind shakes down to a blot
of light. All rules collapse. The green
waves melt against me. We appear
on a November morning and you
unfold me. I belong to you.

Sophia D. Etxeberria

Return to blue

The ocean is cold and blue and rises from sea canyons
to a deep fog that tempers the heat, a heat that breathes
between us, the mountains and the sea, in a dark and scarred
wilderness, scarred like outlaws blown to pieces, bent
on destroying every living thing, dying hard, sexing up
their step-mothers, twisted souls strangled by brooding
danger,
by rat poison. Return to blue.

Waves crash against the shore, slip back into an undertow
of dissatisfaction that paces to the sullen beat of isolation,
swallowed up by the powder of spite, skirting steep, damp
gorges like convicts escaped from hard labor, from hard time,
looking for secret places to be loved, away from the whirring
machines, drifting, searching, clinging to the rock of no
sorrow,
Returning to blue...

By the eleventh hour, the hawks and kingfishers had waged
their war to the death, rebels, lawless inhabitants of the edge
of coastal cliffs,
the Daniel Boones and Abraham Lincolns of all standards,
codes, and conformities that attempt to subvert the wild.

In victory, dragging on sweet port wine, the petty thieves cut
their roads of self-loathing,
despair and delirium into the inland where you and I
once stilled and stopped the world until there was nothing
but blue.

Sai rom (I see the God in you. Hello. Good-bye. I am thankful. Excuse me. Isn't life grand.)

When all the glory of the world has gone to sleep
and the fires have been left alone to weep,

I will sing to you a lover's song.
I will find your eyes clean and deep.

Out of hunger we want for love,
but it is thirst that makes us take the leap.

From the wave of the silent shore
I draw a breath for you to keep

and wait for the hour of the stars
to dream you sighing as we sleep.

Sophia D. Etxeberria

Colorado (for Vincent)

Nothing has changed, nothing.
I stay because of the moon,
for it alone unites the primordial,
so that when it ripens above
the plains, or scatters its light
through the fractured glass
of a skyscraper' it is not then
or never, but now that we drink
each other in with our eyes
shyly lifted from the streets half
lit by the stars. Wild foals drunk
on rich mother's milk.

Here. Listen. A woman opens her shirt
beneath the shadows of sparse grasses
where hooves of stallions pound,
and ravens call, and bees and wasps
hover above dandelions. She opens
with patterns of movement, sweet
like blood, smooth like color.
Silent as sky, she opens her veins.
They pulse with dry heat,
or black dangling seeds
of funnel clouds, or the fat
red of the everywhere, always moon.

Iñaki

We went to look beneath the sea
with the ghosts of horses galloping,
you in your moss green shirt
and wind blown hair, black
and alone under the sky,
breathless with cold fire,
wildness all around and the angels
above, and our dead buried not long ago.
We were galloping, the rumps
of our horses pulsating slightly
in the gray light of dusk
where we floated in the lines
of our hands, and called
to our children from stark cliffs.

Shaking from fatigue and cold,
adorned in rings and bracelets
with my face painted gold,
you drew me in to offer
the warmth of your bed. And the shock
of cold waves, the melancholy
wail of the dog, the black
tongue of the road, the two gypsies
went galloping, reeling,
flying in a circle of dark
rain, falling to the brooding sea,
banished from the stranger, wilder
world of our hearts.

Sophia D. Etxeberria

A letter home

Every morning the sun gets up
to spin the world round and round.
We rise to create in this place we have found.
We spin our dreams
and fill our hearts
and hold on and hold on and hold on until. . .
of a sudden we find ourselves letting go.
All of these things I have believed in,
each one in turn has failed.
Now I'm standing and I'm looking
and this feeling grabs hold.
Your frailness. Your fall. Oh my. Oh my. Oh my.
How could I not love you all?

Sphere

The souls hang low today
whispering through alfalfa
fields in morning fog.
They brush against my lashes,
lay heavy in the road
like stones, shriek
the trill of a swallow.
One, Achuni from Iquitos,
dreams sweet poetry of orchids,
mahogany and rosewood oil trees,
remembers vines along the Peruvian
edge o f the Amazon.
Another from Amoy of southern China
rides the bow of a cargo junk.
His eyes find their way over
pitch dark water.
They are not bound to scenes
of catastrophe. They spread out
through the atmosphere like dark
ribbons of sea water
collecting in bizarre colonies
along the East Pacific Rise,
or the Galapagos Islands,
or lay in shards like dead firecrackers
barely missed by the sad
and lonely face of moonlight.
They seem to swallow the sweet
wine of seasons, drifting through
winter or summer as if here
they might be someone, as if here
they might find their world.

Sophia D. Etxeberria

And even though the sun
rose more than two hours ago,
they are showing me the way.
Through shimmering, gnarled clouds,
black trees
I hear them calling.
They swell, draw apart, reach
through the mist, roll words
across autumn fields like dies.
Listen: This life you are living
is between you and God.

Smile of your memory

Lately, I have been thinking
of you. I suppose because
people have been asking
about you-waiting. We all know
you'll be leaving sooner
than later. You weren't like
the rest of us. Maybe that's why
you are dearer to the heart.
I'm sure of it.

God knows there has been anger
between us, hurt feelings, bad
memories of shared situations
handled like thugs throwing
rocks through windows.
That's about how much we've cared.
But lately I've been thinking
of you. Your cocky grin
indulging in your small
amount of wickedness.

The river is wide. The bridge
is burned. You are on your bank.
I am on mine. But do you see
those swallows flying over us?

Sophia D. Etxeberria

Flocks of memories
of smiles-back and forth
free from the gravity
of everything between us
still saying
"I love you,"
when my voice has been cemented:
buried in resignation
and l no longer hear yours.

That's what l want to remember
you, sitting at my table
laughing.
Smiling.

At your best.
At our best.
I love you.

Sometimes you have to go far away to write a love poem

Hola mi Amor:

In the streets of Pamplona,
I look at the faces of all the people,
alone and together
and I do not see us, you and me,
holding hands,
finding more and more peace
with one another.
We are a man and a woman
who have put down our weapons.
We have wiped away the anger and disappointment
and touched each others scars.
I want to give this to the people in the streets, but I can only carry this feeling in my joints and my bones.
But I feel it. I feel what it is like to make peace with my family, with my origins.
I feel what it is like to return home,
to some part of the world that cast me out long ago. My grandmother left Bizkaia because there was nothing and no one here to hold her. I think of all the Basque who left. I don't have any answers for the big questions and I do have big questions, but I do have you. And when the world and all of her history and the old trees rustle in the wind and the lightning strikes, I think of you wrapping me in your arms, late at night, in the dark. I know you will always hold me when I cry and this is everything I could ever want right now.

Your Dream Lover,
Sophia

Sophia D. Etxeberria

For Xabier-2013

I woke up
  in the middle of the night
    as we passed through the
      straight of Messina.

The mountain roads
  were lit with candelabras.
    Star light, ambient light
      glowed on the horizon.

The moon was
  there too, lying on her
    back. "You are the
      moon," you whispered,

as you pulled back
  to grey sheets
    covered in rose petals,
      infused with dense perfume.

I can still remember
  the velvet rub
    beneath our bodies
      that crushed the red electrons.

In search of God and Haiku

All day the sky was so cold,
birds refused to fly,
until the storm unfurled them.

In frozen creek beds,
Latin chants hibernated,
abandoned by summer.

Cold, dark rhythms,
shadows within shadows,
turtle secrets in ripples.

How elegant the willow whispered,
not like corn gossip,
neighbors none the less.

Sophia D. Etxeberria

The bullfight

There is a canyon in southern Wyoming. The closest town in any direction is an hour's drive on a dirt road. In the winter it is filled with snow and howling wind. In the summer there is just enough grass, barely enough rain, and never too much of anything except the wind and the sun. Only the wildest animals can live there. They take shelter and forage in forests. It is a hard country. It is a battleground whose beauty is complete.

Every morning the sun comes up and drags its pale light into the Wyoming arena, the same routine that has taken place for eons. In the summer, light sweeps across every green blade and the blue drops of stream water. It moves into shadows under the leaves. And finally, when all things have been touched, the heat and light spreads open and glares down on the animals until their blood begins to simmer.

Elk and deer take refuge in the shade of aspen groves that grow along the upper edges of the canyon. Antelope, horses, and sheep weave in and out of service trees and willows. Badgers scurry along paths that lead to deep, cool holes. Coyotes, bears, and rattlesnakes shade-up, but the cattle stay on the floor of the canyon grazing, twitching, and flinching as flies bite their backs.

Calves nuzzle udders for milk while here and there a cow stands to breed. The cows are coming in and out of heat. The bulls barely have time to eat. They are exhausted. They follow the cows with their lips curled up, delirious from the scent that wafts through the canyon, irritable from breeding beneath the hot sky. By late afternoon a Black Angus and a white Charolais are locked in a head-to-head battle.

Their muscles strain against the power of one another. They push forward, retreat, and then spin. Dust flies up around their flanks. The bulls crash through the sagebrush, stumbling, bellowing, but never surrendering their positions. Their roars echo up and down the canyon.

One lone hawk circles above. She sweeps down and with smooth precision, her talons enclose around a scurrying chipmunk. The bulls circle, pawing, kicking the dirt. A gust of wind tumbles down the canyon, rippling the willows along the banks of the stream. The bulls paw the dirt and bellow in fury. A rattler strikes and misses, then quickly coils itself around the trunk of a sage. The bulls dig in deeper, forcing their heads against one another.

Calves come running. They are gamblers kicking up their heels and vying for front row seats, scooting around to study every move. The white Charolais stumbles and crashes. The calves jump back, making room for the fighters. Another bull, a young, red Simmental pushes through the calves, discovers the fight, and waits for a break. He circles round and round, but the white and the black are locked in battle. The three bulls crash up against the calves, scream, tear the earth with their powerful hooves. Their nostrils flare and the dust envelops them in a thick cloud. Their muscles flex and ripple beneath their hides. The black and the white jut out from one another like strokes of Picasso. The red circles in a fury, bellowing, bellowing, until the cows come running, females in heat, red and black and white, females with calves. They circle round and round.

The cows push the calves away for a better view. The cows bellow. The bulls scream. The calves bleat. The canyon walls are filled with echoes. Dust boils higher and higher. A magpie hops along at a safe distance, scolding and jabbering about the violence. Then, far above it all from some distance up the canyon, the roar of a bull rips down the middle of the chaos and the mayhem. It is the roar of the primero bull. An 1800-pound grand jefe, the biggest and oldest bull of them all. The red Hereford bull sniffs the air and rears up on his hind legs to mount a black cow that is standing in heat, waiting to breed, and then the Hereford lunges.

All things eventually come to an end. The white Charolais finally turns aside. He takes a hit in the shoulder and then grumbles off down a path to follow the tail of a red and white cow. The red Simmental and the Black Angus are similarly distracted as the dust settles and the image of cows emerges before them. An elegant old Hereford arrives, but by now the dust has fallen and calves are back to nuzzling udders. He swings his powerful head from side to side and then with one sharp eye he spots the Simmental, the youngest bull, mounted on the hind flanks of a black cow with one white patch around her nose. The Hereford's powerful legs explode, and with one clean hit he knocks the Simmental to the ground. The young bull scrambles to his feet. His eyes roll back and he shudders. His lips part slowly and then from the depth of his groin he releases a terrible, choking moan. He stumbles, one leg buckles. He takes a few steps, and then collapses beneath a willow by the stream just as the night locks the canyon into darkness.

A storm moves in from the southwest. There is no moonlight, no brilliant stars, only thick black clouds that rumble. The pain throbs. He moans and pants, with his head on the dirt. In the distance a pack of coyotes howl. Behind his back the bushes rustle. A jackrabbit lopes by on his way to water. The storm cracks. Lightning strikes all around. To the south, sharp and angular and vivid. To the west, broad and long above the rim of the canyon. A slight rain falls, just enough to settle the dust and freshen the grass, but not enough to keep the plants from withering under tomorrow's sun.

The bull lies with one eye to the sky, unable to escape the pain, unable to escape the terror of the electric. Oh where, oh where is a good cowboy when you need him?

In the morning, the sun comes up and drags out its pale light. The Simmental moans and pants and twitches his tail at the flies that gather around his broken, exposed, and swollen maleness. He pulls himself up from the dirt; stumbles to the stream with his head slumped down, waiting for the slow monotony of heat to guide him through the day. Days turn into night and darkness into light, and for two weeks the bull rises and falls in the battleground beneath the sun.

At first it sounds like a whistle of wind and thin like the twinkle of a finch's song. But then the Simmental hears it clearly. It is a familiar sound that cuts through his agony. It is the voice of Demetrio singing his songs from the back of his mare, Cat Balou.

"Me gusto por la mañana..."

The voice draws nearer... and nearer... until the cowboy and the mare stand above the injured bull. The Simmental tries to pull himself up, but the pain anchors him into the dirt. The cowboy gets off the mare and ties her to a willow. He circles and squats and tips his head from side to side. He spits into the dirt and swears. Then he stands up, walks to his horse, and withdraws a Remington 243 from the leather case strapped to the side of his saddle. He aims right between the bull's eyes and fires and the bull's head falls by the water beneath the wind and the sun.

Este libro se terminó de imprimir
el 11 de septiembre de 2015

www.ingramcontent.com/pod-product-compliance
Lightning Source LLC
Chambersburg PA
CBHW020904090426
42736CB00008B/491